THE 3,000TH HIT

by Gloria Gorman
illustrated by Sam Day

Harcourt

Orlando   Boston   Dallas   Chicago   San Diego

Visit *The Learning Site!*

www.harcourtschool.com

Above the Pittsburgh Airport fly
My brothers, my papa, and I.
The control tower's in our sight.
My heart is happy and so light.

The wonder we are here to see
Is famed Roberto Clemente.
How must he feel this final hour?
We're signaled by the control tower...

Clemente! He's a shining star.
He summons fans from near and far
To watch him play this special game
Called baseball, even in this rain!

We find the ballpark—hearts aglow.
Oh! Will he do it? Do you know?
There he is. I see his hat.
He's in the lineup, next to bat.

I'm in that lineup with our ace.
I'm practice-swinging in his place!
The artificial turf will be
Where we meet our destiny.

It is no error we are here.
We're dedicated, it is clear.
Everyone is tensing up.
The umpire calls out, "Batter up!"

Clemente! What a special ace!
Perhaps today he'll make his place
Among the best who play this game.
Then everyone will know his name!

The crowd is still. The air is, too.
What will this ace, Clemente, do?
He steps right up. He's at the plate.
I feel it in my bones—it's fate.

My heart is racing, wild and fast.
The moment—it has come at last.
A hit! A hit that hits the wall!
No error will this umpire call.

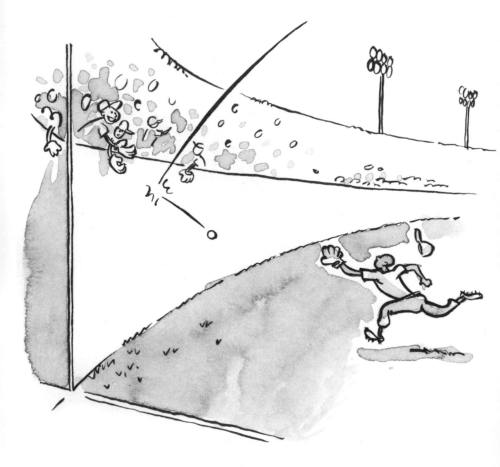

He drops the bat. He runs the race.
Roberto is on second base!
The fans go wild with crazy screams.
Roberto has fulfilled his dreams.

The joy explodes in shouts so loud
As rapture thunders through the crowd.
For sixty seconds, shouting goes.
Applause, applause—and on it flows.

Clemente! What a special ace!
No other man can take his place.
He did not falter, did not quit.
He made that great 3,000th hit.

On artificial turf he stood—
An athlete splendid, great, and good.
He tasted victory so sweet.
He watched us jumping to our feet.

We're going home so thunderstruck.
We know that hit was not pure luck.
How dedicated he must be.
He earned his place in history.

Clemente—his will be the name
Inducted into Hall of Fame.
His name remembered, sea to sea.
And I was there to see it . . . me!